GATEWAY TO AMERICA
LIBERTY ISLAND AND ELLIS ISLAND

SMITHMARK

This edition first published in 1992 by SMITHMARK
Publishers Inc., 112 Madison Avenue,
New York, New York 10016

ISBN 0-8317-3768-9

Printed and bound in Spain

Writer: Nancy Millichap Davies
Designer: Ann-Louise Lipman
Design Concept: Lesley Ehlers
Editor: Joan E. Ratajack
Production: Valerie Zars
Photo Researcher: Edward Douglas
Assistant Photo Researcher: Robert V. Hale
Editorial Assistant: Carol Raguso

Title page: A pleasure craft with canvas lowered glides toward the Statue of Liberty at sunset, recalling the days of sail. *Opposite:* A skewed perspective makes Lady Liberty appear to tower above the restored immigration station on neighboring Ellis Island. *Overleaf:* The Statue of Liberty—a weathered copper presence against lower Manhattan's glittering skyline.

Since the last years of the nineteenth century, maritime traffic approaching the port of New York has sailed by two structures that represent important facets of the United States' culture and ideals. Although the Statue of Liberty and the Ellis Island Immigration Station have their own distinct histories, their sites on adjacent islands in New York Harbor have created a powerful association between them, particularly in the minds of immigrants. To the millions of new arrivals who first saw the towering torchbearer on Bedloe's Island at the end of a long, difficult voyage, she embodied their new country. Trials to be passed under the lofty figure's very shadow in Ellis Island's halls would determine whether they might remain in her realm. The two grand constructions came to represent the scale of the American dream and, for hopeful newcomers from all over the world, a way station on their road toward achieving it.

Like so much that has come to be regarded as the essence of the American way, the Statue of Liberty was conceived and created in Europe. The idea that was to become the reality of Lady Liberty dawned in the years just after the Civil War that had threatened, but failed, to break the union of North and South. French liberals of the 1860's saw the United States as a nation that had achieved their goal: stable democracy. One evening at a dinner in his home, liberal leader Edward Laboulaye mentioned his idea of creating a monument to liberty as a gift to the United States from the

Preceding page: Above Liberty's stern face, her crown is pierced by windows from which visitors gaze after climbing an interior staircase. *This page, top to bottom:* An unusual close-up shows the rear of Liberty's hair and crown. Roman numerals on the tablet in the statue's hand give the official birth date of the United States: July 4, 1776. Appearing to flow like cloth, the Lady's copper skirts sweep her 89-foot pedestal.

people of France on the occasion of the younger nation's 100th birthday in 1876. One of Laboulaye's guests was an ambitious young sculptor, Frédéric-Auguste Bartholdi. Under the influence of his travels among Egypt's imposing monuments, Bartholdi had already designed and roughly modeled *Egypt Bringing the Light to Asia*. He designed the 75-foot female figure with a torch to serve as a lighthouse at the entrance to the Suez Canal. Egypt's ruler, however, rejected the plan. Now an even more splendid opportunity presented itself to the artist's imagination. For New York Harbor, which he described as "the entrance of that vast continent, full of life, where ships meet from all points of the world," he modeled a woman's form twice as big as his original statue.

To carry out their extraordinary project, Bartholdi and Laboulaye needed money. In 1875, Laboulaye and the French-American Union he headed set about raising it. There were fund-raising events throughout Paris, from gala dinners to benefit performances at the opera. Ordinary citizens as well as the wealthy contributed. Simultaneously, Bartholdi began the complex process of creating Miss Liberty in the Paris workshops of Gaget, Gauthier et Cie. To realize the sculptor's design, workers under his direction used three exact models of increasing sizes 4, 9, and 37 feet high. Projecting from the last and largest complete model, they made plaster sections of actual size and then copied these with elaborate wooden skeletons upon which to re-create each section in copper. They spread plates of copper within the wooden molds and hand-hammered them into shape, adding

Top: Dusk: The Statue of Liberty's torch throws out a 13,000-watt gleam from 305 feet above sea level. *Left:* Liberty's 151-foot height is a compelling site against an evening sky. *Opposite:* Fireworks on July 4, 1986, celebrated her 100th birthday.

Preceding pages: Brilliant illumination against spectacular sunset colors makes the Statue of Liberty the focus of this New York Harbor scene. *This page:* Ellis Island, largely composed of landfill added little by little over the years, occupies 27½ acres of New York Harbor.

strength and thinning the metal at the same time. This ancient metal-working method, called repouss, produced a shell 3/32 of an inch thick in 350 separate sections, each shaped precisely to Bartholdi's design.

Even so, the shell as a whole weighed some 200,000 pounds. French bridge engineer Gustave Eiffel, who would later create Paris's Eiffel Tower, designed a way of supporting it against even powerful harbor winds by transferring its weight to a sturdy interior frame-work. A tower of four massive wrought-iron pylons supported diagonally braced iron struts, which in turn supported flat iron bars. These bars were connected to iron straps fastened directly to the copper skin. Workers erected Eiffel's pylons in the workshop's yard. As each copper section was completed, they attached it to the frame. Startling contemporary images show Liberty encased in scaffolding towering over the five-story apartment buildings near her birthplace.

Laboulaye and Bartholdi had received assurances from their American contacts that the people of the United States would raise funds to create a foundation and pedestal for the statue. To inspire their gifts, Bartholdi created the statue's upraised arm and torch first and brought them to the United States in time for the 1876 centennial celebration in Philadelphia. Even with this evidence of the glory to be, fund-raising proved a slow business. Neither New York's fabulously wealthy entrepreneurs nor the state government contributed very freely. In the end, it was news-paper publisher Joseph Pulitzer, a

Top: Opened in 1900, the Ellis Island Immigration Station was the first stop for most newcomers over the next half century. *Right:* Its four-towered main building was restored between 1984 and 1990 at a cost of $160 million.

Ellis Island's Art Deco Ferry Building (above) and its hospital complex (below) still await restoration.

On their approach to the Registry Building, visitors pass under a contemporary canopy added during the recent renovations. *Below:* The canopy's supports and rails, their shadows, and the façade beyond form striking geometric patterns.

Hungarian immigrant, who led a successful campaign in the pages of his newspaper, the *New York World*. Many of the contributions the *World* received came from men and women of limited means who were eager to receive France's gift in the generous spirit in which it was given. Richard Morris Hunt, the period's most popular architect, designed an 89-foot pedestal for the statue that rose within the base of an old fort on Bedloe's Island in New York Harbor. (The site has since been renamed Liberty Island.)

In June 1885, the French ship *Isère* arrived in New York flying a hundred flags and carrying the disassembled statue, but the pedestal was not completed until the following April. During the summer of 1886, workers in wooden seats on cables glided up and down, attaching bars to framework and copper sheets to bars, and joining the sheets permanently with a total of more than 300,000 copper rivets. October 28, 1886 was a cold and rainy day in New York, but it did not stop the parade of 20,000 marchers nor the thousands who lined the harbor to see the veil—a French tricolor—lifted from Liberty's face.

Independence Day weekend 1986 was equally festive on and around Liberty Island. There were two reasons to celebrate: Liberty's 100th birthday, and the completion of major repairs to counteract the effects of a century of wet, windy exposure. The renovation included replacement of the torch and of the 1,600 iron straps that hold the copper sheeting to the interior framework. The two-year project also added an interior elevator that

Top: A modern deck for outdoor dining contrasts with the Registry Building's turn-of-the-century design. *Left:* Trim within trim, metal grillwork patterns a limestone-edged Registry Building portal.

THE AMERICAN IMMIGRANT WALL OF HONOR

The Wall of Honor has sustained some damage because of vandalism and the
environmental elements. The Statue of Liberty-Ellis Island Foundation is
testing new and stronger sealants. The Foundation wants all Wall supporters
to be aware that when the tests are completed, the Wall will be repaired.

Damage to Federal property is subject to a fine.

A sign near the Wall of Honor, which lists the names of many of the nation's immigrants, suggests that it is, in several ways, a work in progress. *Below:* Slanting late-day light emphasizes the symmetry of the façade's detail.

makes the viewing area in the crown accessible to those unable to climb the 335 steps within the pedestal and statue. As a highlight of the four-day festival, more than 200 tall ships passed before the statue in a 4-mile-long Parade of Sail on that Fourth of July.

Through the blowing whistles and cannon smoke of the 1886 celebration, according to a newspaper of the day, sailed a ship crowded with European immigrants. For them, and for the millions who would follow them into New York Harbor, the statue was the focal point of their first view of America: magnificent, strange, larger than life. Within six years, immigrants' first steps on American soil would take place on nearby Ellis Island. The statue designed to embody the link between French and American political ideals would, over time, become an icon of the United States itself, and especially of its promise to the immigrant of a place to start anew.

The region of North America that would one day be called the United States was a land of immigrants from its first days of human habitation. Even the people known today as native Americans originally crossed to the continent from Asia. In the period of European discovery, settlers from the exploring nations formed colonies along the coasts. The inhabitants of the East Coast cities who ultimately revolted against Britain to form

Preceding page: One of the Registry Building's four 100-foot domed towers. *This page:* Limestone carvings of a classical head over a portal (top) and an eagle and shield at the top of a pilaster (right) proclaim the building's Beaux Arts origins.

an independent nation in the late 1700's were, for the most part, of British descent. But by that time there was also a significant German-speaking population in the British colonies, consisting mainly of farmers who had come from the southwestern portion of today's Germany seeking religious freedom and good farmland in Pennsylvania.

In addition, about a million African-Americans lived in the United States by 1800. Almost all of them, or their ancestors, had been enslaved and forced to emigrate from Africa. This forced migration ended in 1808, when the slave trade was abolished, although enslavement of African-Americans already in the country continued until 1863.

The immigrants of the first century following the American Revolution continued to come largely from the European countries that had supplied the original settlers: England, Scotland, Wales, Ulster (now Northern Ireland), and the various lands along the Rhine that became Germany in 1870. But in the middle 1800's, powerful forces at work in Europe led to changes in the pattern of immigration. Europe's population was increasing rapidly because of improvements in health care. At the same time, political and industrial revolutions were changing patterns of employment and driving farmers off the land. The Irish potato famine of the 1840's led thousands of Irish farmers to leave home, sometimes on unsafe vessels, in their desperation to escape starvation and to find work. As hungry

Top: Immigrants were encouraged to leave their belongings in this baggage room, but often refused and carried them along throughout their lengthy examinations. *Left:* Heaps of period luggage and photographs in the baggage room recall its original use. *Opposite:* A richly patterned carpetbag sits atop trunks bearing Welsh and German names.

The varying textures of metal, wood, wicker, and leather luggage add rugged contrast to this display. *Below:* A well-worn trunk suggests the rigors of an immigrant's sea journey. *Opposite:* A neglected baggage cart rusts before sturdy chests of the kind it once transported.

Preceding page: Registry Hall, or the Great Hall, is where examiners, standing at desks below this flag, began their questioning. *This page, above:* The 160-foot-long registry room with its lofty ceiling was the largest that many of the foreigners had ever entered. *Below:* Immigrants sat on these benches awaiting the first of a series of examinations.

Preceding page: Following in immigrant footsteps, a group of visitors passes
one of the offices above Registry Hall where examinations were also conducted.
This page: Here, a Registry Office window frame imprints a distinctive grid on
the lower Manhattan skyline across the harbor.

and often physically ill crowds poured into New York, site of the nation's largest port, it became obvious to state officials that they needed some policies for dealing with the newcomers.

In 1855, New York State opened the first immigration station anywhere in a one-time military fort called Castle Garden just off the southern tip of Manhattan. Compassion was one important motive for its establishment. Dishonest money-changers, boardinghouse operators, and women of uncertain reputation were all too likely to meet the immigrant ships and take full advantage of the new arrivals' innocence. Also, Castle Garden provided both a place to record the names and ports of origin of the prospective immigrants and a chance to quarantine those who carried dangerous diseases or turn back those who lacked means to support themselves. For immigrants, Castle Garden offered services regulated by the government, at least while they were within its walls, rather than by the many spurious characters anxious to profit at their expense.

Regrettably, profiteering of another kind flourished at Castle Garden. Corrupt state officials manipulated the services offered to make money for themselves. In addition, the limited dimensions of the old offshore fort could not long handle the growing volume of newcomers. Throughout Europe, "America fever" was spreading as the first immigrants found work in the growing nation and sent back reports—and money. Increasingly, immigrants came from regions other than those of the colonial settlers, as the social and industrial changes that had affected northern

Top: The "Guastavino" ceiling of the Great Hall, named for the immigrant Italian brothers who devised the basket-weave tilework style, was installed in 1920. *Left:* The room's chandeliers date from the same period.

and western Europe spread world-wide. The men and women arriving at the end of the nineteenth century were from Italy, the Slavic nations, and, increasingly, from the *shtetls*—agricultural Jewish villages—of Russia, as their inhabitants began to be the targets of pogroms, or campaigns of violent repression. Smaller groups arrived from many other nations: Syrians from the Middle East, Armenians and Indians from Asia, people of African and native American descent from the Caribbean, and Filipinos, especially after World War I.

Immigration for the five-year period preceding the 1855 opening of Castle Garden was just under 1,750,000. During the five years before the Statue of Liberty was unveiled in 1886, almost 3 million arrived. About 80 percent of those people passed through the port of New York. A new and much larger immigration station, designed especially for the purpose, was obviously needed to handle the flood of those who would come to be called the "new immigrants."

The dramatic increase in immigration alarmed some who were already in the the United States. The newcomers, they alleged, were stealing jobs from the "old immigrants" and changing the prevailing Anglo-Saxon patterns of the national culture. In response to such charges, Congress put some curbs on immigration. In 1882, it passed a law that prohibited "any convict, lunatic, idiot, or any person unable to take care of himself or herself without becoming a public charge" or anyone suffering from a "loathsome or contagious disease." (Two previous laws restricted

Top: Inspectors kept a sharp lookout for physical problems as immigrants climbed these Registry Building stairs. *Right:* Sunlight floods the Great Hall, a place of great anxiety during the years of immigration.

Lord & Taylor holiday windows depict the Ellis Island Registry Building adorned with garlands and lights; mannequins represent immigrant families.

Ellis's "Through America's Gate" exhibits include the medical and psychological tests given to immigrants. A period photo (above, right) shows the dreaded eye exam.

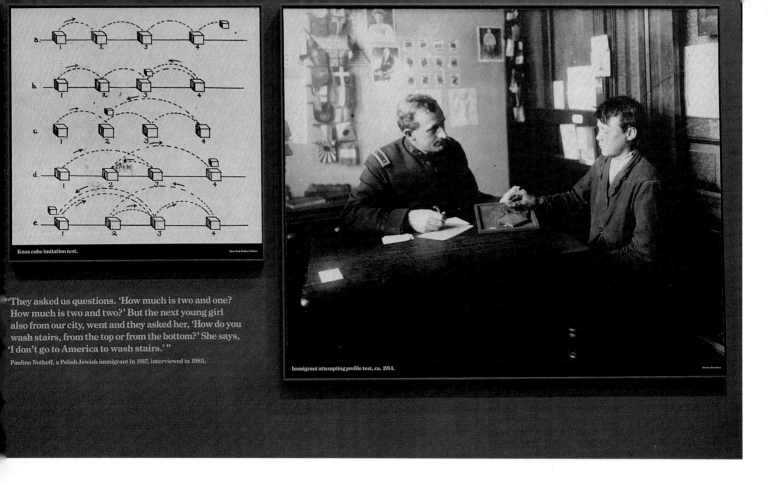

"They asked us questions. 'How much is two and one? How much is two and two?' But the next young girl also from our city, went and they asked her, 'How do you wash stairs, from the top or from the bottom?' She says, 'I don't go to America to wash stairs.'"

Pauline Notkoff, a Polish Jewish immigrant in 1917, interviewed in 1985.

Knox cube imitation test. / New York Public Library

Immigrant attempting profile test, ca. 1914. / Brown Brothers

Above: In an exhibit photo, a boy takes a mental test designed to spot the "feeble-minded." *Below, left:* In this exhibit, visitors see various results of one mental test question, "draw a diamond." *Right:* Ellis Island saw the drama of human life from cradle to grave.

Mental Testing

By 1917, immigration laws prohibited the admission of all aliens diagnosed as suffering from any mental impairment. The immigrant population's wide variety of educational and cultural backgrounds, however, made assessing individual intelligence extremely difficult. To screen new arrivals, Ellis Island doctors used standard intelligence tests as well as tests they developed themselves in an attempt to deal with these cultural differences. Doctors based their decisions on their subject's level of acquired knowledge, problem-solving ability, behavior, and attitude.

Perla Katz gave birth to her son in the Ellis Island hospital.

Records dating from 1900 show that over 3,500 people, including more than 1,400 children, died on Ellis Island. Burials were arranged by either friends or relatives, charity associations, or, as a last resort, by an undertaker contracted by the Immigration Service. Though death was a far more frequent occurrence, births too were part of the hospital routine. Over 355 babies were born on Ellis Island.

Birth and Death

immigrants from China, who had entered the United States primarily through ports on the Pacific coast.) An inspection at the port of entry established whether a prospective immigrant fit any of the prohibited categories. Shipowners who had brought those who were not admitted would have to pay for their transportation back to their port of origin.

In 1885, another law intended to protect American workers excluded immigrants called "contract laborers," effectively ending the days when employers could draw up contracts with immigrants before they arrived, as they had in the colonial days when indentured servants worked seven years to repay their passage money. At about the same time, the federal government took over control of immigration from the individual states, including New York. Castle Garden's replacement would be a federal facility.

As its site, officials selected 3-acre Ellis Island. New Yorkers had gathered oysters there in the early days of settlement, and during the War of 1812 Ellis Island, like Bedloe's Island, had been the site of a fort. In the 1880's, landfill doubled the size of the island to make room for the new station. A complex of Georgia pine buildings including a three-story main depot rose in 1892. In the first year of operation, 450,000 arrivals taxed its capacities. For the rest of the 1890's, though, the United States was in an economic slump, and immigration levels dropped off sharply. In 1897, the Ellis Island buildings burned completely to the ground. By a stroke of luck, no lives were lost, but all the records of Castle Garden immigration were destroyed.

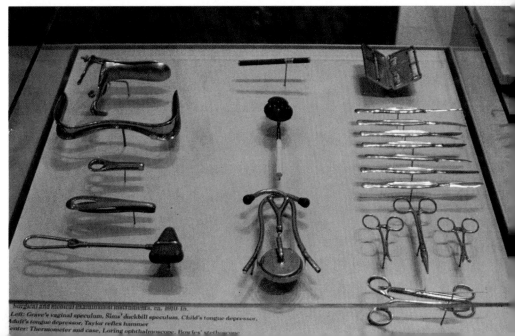

Top: A period photograph of the island's hospital serves as a backdrop for an early wheelchair. *Right:* Implements from a medical examiner's tool kit dominate this exhibit.

Therefore, the decreased numbers of immigrants during the 1890's were used as the basis for projecting future immigration when the construction of a new, fireproof complex began. The second Ellis Island station opened with the century in 1900 and was designed to process 5,000 arrivals a day. But in its first decade of operation more than 6 million immigrants passed through. Ellis Island officials handled 1,004,756 arrivals in 1907, the peak year.

For most of its years of operation, Ellis Island processed only those immigrants who had traveled in "steerage," ships' lowest decks, on relatively inexpensive tickets. Immigration officials examined first- and cabin-class passengers aboard ship, after which barges took the steerage passengers to the immigration station. Once on the island, newcomers entered the reception building, stowed their baggage on the first level, and headed upstairs for the medical inspection.

Most were unaware of it, but until the main stairway was moved in 1911, medical inspectors were making a preliminary observation known as the "6-second medical" as they ascended. Doctors in the Registry Hall at the top of the stairs continued the inspection, chalking letters on the clothing of immigrants they wished to examine more thoroughly. An "L" meant possible lameness and an "E" potential eye trouble, for example. Those whose problems could not be dismissed in a two- to three-minute examination were detained at government expense for further examination and perhaps

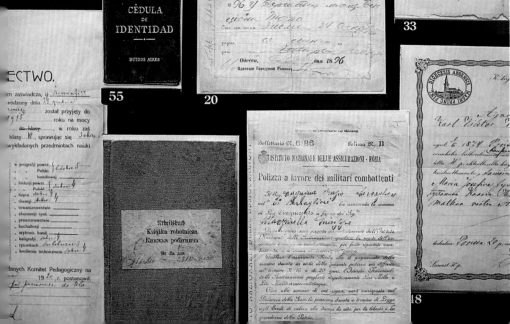

Top: This document testifies to an Englishwoman's good conduct. *Left:* Immigrants' papers suggest the diversity of languages they spoke.

Multilingual graffiti (above) and a sketch of a water bird (below) still remain on a men's dormitory wall.

Stout wire before a photograph of detainees (above and below, left) recalls the immigrants who were held on the island for further testing. Only 2 percent were ultimately refused admission. *Below, right:* Officials who determined detainees' fates sat at these desks to deliberate. *Opposite:* A detainees' dormitory: Privacy was not a feature.

Preceding page: Detained immigrants ate their first American meals, served on tableware like this, in Ellis's dining rooms. *This page, above:* In a dark interior sits office equipment of a bygone era. *Below:* Some Ellis Island interiors, like this inspection room, still await restoration.

Maps combine with photographs in this exhibit to give a sense of immigrants' origins and journeys. *Below:* A dramatic look down a Registry Room stairwell gives a sense of the building's height.

treatment for a few days to as much as two weeks. Because they sometimes ended in exclusion of an immigrant from the country or, perhaps even more terribly, the separation of families, these detentions led to great anxiety.

After the medical, immigrants waited in long lines for questioning by the 20 primary inspectors, who had the power to exclude or admit on the basis of their own findings and the results of the medical inspection. Immigrants not speaking English answered the questions through Ellis Island's interpreters, who were fluent in a total of 30 languages. About 80 percent of the immigrants were admitted at this stage. The remainder were detained to go before boards of special inquiry because of questions about their physical or mental fitness or ability to support themselves, or about whether they represented contract labor.

Ellis Island had sleeping accommodations for 1,500 people, but often more than 2,000 were being temporarily detained. At such times, some slept on the Registry Hall's hard wooden benches. Overall, approximately 2 percent of those who came to Ellis Island (that's about 240,000 people between 1892 and 1954) were denied entry to the United States and sent back. Although the percentage is small, it explains why so many pictures of arriving immigrants show people whose expressions range from solemn to deeply anxious. Beneath the bustle, the excitement of new beginnings, and the brilliance of the national costume that many immigrants wore on their first day on U.S. soil, Ellis Island had frightening overtones of Judgment Day.

Here at the "kissing post," families came together in a new land.

Building History

"The Kissing Post"

In this area, immigrants were reunited with waiting friends and relatives who had preceded them to America. The emotional and joyous scenes that took place here prompted an Ellis Island matron to write the following in 1910: "The manner in which the people of different nationalities greet each other after a separation of years is one of the interesting studies at the Island. The Italian kisses his little children but scarcely speaks to his wife, never embraces or kisses her in public. The Hungarian and Slavish [sic] people put their arms around one another and weep. The Jew of all countries kisses his wife and children as though he had all the kisses in the world, and intended to use them all up quick."

A telegram and period photographs suggest the relief of admitted immigrants finally heading across to Manhattan. *Below:* This display shows examples of the foreign currencies that were exchanged for American dollars.

Above: Many U.S. destinations tempted the new arrivals. *Below, left:* Signboards suggest jobs available to immigrant laborers and skilled tradesmen, at the wages of an earlier era. *Right:* Railroad companies beckoned the newcomers to states across the country.

Preceding page: An arrangement of contemporary photographs of Ellis Island immigrants' descendants takes on the expression of the American flag. *This page:* Descendants of Ellis Island immigrants include 100 million Americans, 40 percent of the nation's people.

Illuminated trails on an exhibit globe mark the movement of various populations from land to land over the centuries. *Below:* A tree of words shows some of the thousands that have come into the English language from other tongues.

A map of the country's growth suggests the need for settlers in the vast American West, a condition that encouraged immigration. *Below:* In this three-dimensional graph of immigration patterns, colors represent countries of origin.

1961–
1980

1941–
1960

1921–
1940

1901–
1920

1881–
1900

1861–
1880

This map lets visitors see the percentages of various ethnic groups in each state. *Below:* These figures represent the proportions of men and women in the immigrant population over the decades.

These pages: Precious memories: Linens, laces, and garments on display and recorded in period photographs suggest the rich handicraft and needlework traditions of the immigrants' countries of origin.

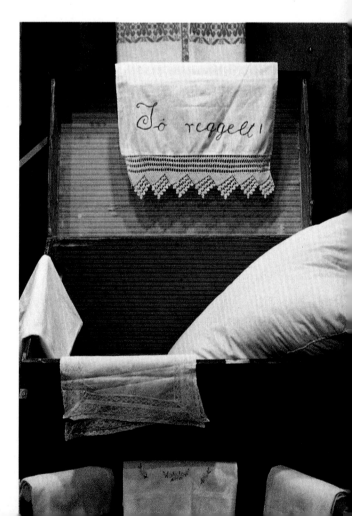

After 1918, immigration never again reached the high levels of the years before World War I. The voices that had led to the restrictions on immigration in the 1880's grew louder and prevailed. A "gentleman's agreement" with Japan in 1908, under which the Japanese agreed to screen and limit the number of their citizens who would receive passports, ended most immigration from that island nation. Strict quotas based on the national origins of those seeking entry that favored the northern European nations of the old immigrants became law in the 1920's. The combined effect of this quota system and the depression of the 1930's sharply reduced immigration, making Ellis Island's elaborate facilities outmoded. After World War II, most immigrants made their arrangements and were admitted by American consulates in their countries of origin.

With over 7 million people immigrating to the United States in the last 20 years, the golden door is again open. Immigration policy has seen several revisions since the restrictive laws of the 1920's. Those laws changed substantially after World War II, especially regarding the admission of those from nations outside Europe. Immigration from the Far East resumed, in small numbers at first, after the Chinese Exclusion Acts were repealed in 1943. Barriers against Latinos fell, giving new importance to north-south immigration within the Western Hemisphere. Gradually, the criteria for admission came to focus less on the national origin of the immigrant and more upon his or her level of education and skill.

National costumes were frequently worn by immigrants on the day they landed at Ellis Island. A closer view (left) reveals deep colors and lush textures. *Opposite:* A German child's teddy bear wears a handmade outfit.

36

Preceding pages: Prized possessions in the "Treasures from Home" exhibit include a Jewish prayer shawl (left) and zither and candelabrum (right). *This page, above:* Rosaries, crucifixes, and a sacred text are set before a backdrop of fine textiles. *Below:* A wide-ranging collection in "Treasures from Home" includes dishes, utensils, and kitchen implements (right). *Opposite:* Immigrants' Bibles in their own languages are displayed in this extraordinary exhibit.

Preceding page: In a striking black-and-white image, admitted immigrants gaze toward Lady Liberty. *This page:* Before a panoramic lower Manhattan skyline, visitors examine the Wall of Honor with its records of immigrants' names etched in copper.

Panel 022
Bai-Bal

Panel 023
Bal-Ban

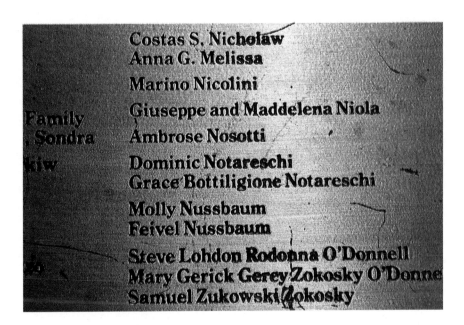

Costas S. Nicholaw
Anna G. Melissa

Marino Nicolini

Giuseppe and Maddelena Niola

Family   Ambrose Nosotti
Sondra

kiw   Dominic Notareschi
               Grace Bottiligione Notareschi

               Molly Nussbaum
               Feivel Nussbaum

               Steve Lohdon Rodonna O'Donnell
               Mary Gerick Gerey Zokosky O'Donne
               Samuel Zukowski Zokosky

Hundreds of thousands of immigrants'
names are listed alphabetically in family
groupings on the Wall of Honor.

Meanwhile a few people still stayed in Ellis Island's once-crowded halls in its last years. Immigrants about to be expelled, either because they had entered the country illegally or had committed a crime, awaited deportation there. During World War II, they were joined by citizens of the nations with which the United States was at war, as well as personnel from enemy ships being held in U.S. ports. After the war, some of the 400,000 European refugees admitted to the United States under the Displaced Persons Act came through Ellis Island. Although the island's population averaged only about 600 by the late 1940's, the station captured national attention again in 1950 when 1,500 suspected Fascists and Communists were detained there at the beginning of the Korean conflict. But in 1953 there were only 230 detainees under the care of the island's 250 staff members. In 1954, immigration officials left the island.

Ellis Island became a national monument in 1965. After decades of deterioration, the island's main building was extensively restored at a cost of $160 million and opened to the public as the Ellis Island Immigration Museum in 1990. In floor space, it is among New York's largest museums. Since it is estimated that almost half the people in the United States today are the descendants of Ellis Island immigrants, it is likely to remain a popular attraction for years to come.

Top: A visitor makes a rubbing of a name at the Wall of Honor. *Left:* Another takes notes of names from the roll of immigrants. *Opposite:* The immigrant experience captured in a single image: the Wall of Honor, the Statue of Liberty, and the American flag fluttering above it all.

Index of Photography

All photographs courtesy of The Image Bank except where indicated *.